IMPROVING SENSORY PROCESSING
IN TRAUMATIZED CHILDREN

of related interest

Can I tell you about Sensory Processing Difficulties?
A guide for friends, family and professionals
Sue Allen
Illustrated by Mike Medaglia
ISBN 978 1 84905 640 3
eISBN 978 1 78450 137 2

The Pocket Occupational Therapist for Families
of Children With Special Needs
Cara Koscinski
ISBN 978 1 84905 932 9
eISBN 978 0 85700 721 6

Fuzzy Buzzy Groups for Children with Developmental
and Sensory Processing Difficulties
A Step-by-Step Resource
Fiona Brownlee and Lindsay Munro
Illustrated by Aisling Nolan
ISBN 978 1 84310 966 2
eISBN 978 0 85700 194 8

The Kids' Guide to Staying Awesome and In Control
Simple Stuff to Help Children Regulate their Emotions and Senses
Lauren Brukner
ISBN 978 1 84905 997 8
eISBN 978 0 85700 962 3

Games and Activities for Attaching With Your Child
Deborah D. Gray and Megan Clarke
ISBN 978 1 84905 795 0
eISBN 978 1 78450 152 5

Promoting Attachment With a Wiggle, Giggle, Hug and Tickle
A Programme for Babies, Young Children and Carers
Fiona Brownlee and Lindsay Norris
ISBN 978 1 84905 656 4
eISBN 978 1 78450 149 5

Attaching Through Love, Hugs and Play
Simple Strategies to Help Build Connections with Your Child
Deborah D. Gray
ISBN 978 1 84905 939 8
eISBN 978 0 85700 753 7

IMPROVING SENSORY PROCESSING IN TRAUMATIZED CHILDREN

Practical Ideas to Help Your Child's Movement, Co-ordination and Body Awareness

SARAH LLOYD

Jessica Kingsley *Publishers*
London and Philadelphia

First published in 2016
by Jessica Kingsley Publishers
73 Collier Street
London N1 9BE, UK
and
400 Market Street, Suite 400
Philadelphia, PA 19106, USA

www.jkp.com

Library of Congress Cataloging in Publication Data
Names: Lloyd, Sarah, 1967- author.
Title: Improving sensory processing in traumatized children : simple ideas to
    help your child's movement, coordination and body awareness / Sarah Lloyd.
Description: London ; Philadelphia : Jessica Kingsley Publishers, 2016. |
    Includes bibliographical references and index.
Identifiers: LCCN 2015027858 | ISBN 9781785920042 (alk. paper)
Subjects: LCSH: Abused children--Rehabilitation. | Sensory disorders in
    children--Patients--Rehabilitation.
Classification: LCC RJ507.A29 L56 2016 | DDC
618.92/8--dc23 LC record available at
http://lccn.loc.gov/2015027858

British Library Cataloguing in Publication Data
A CIP catalogue record for this book is available from the British Library

ISBN 978 1 78592 004 2
eISBN 978 1 78450 239 3

Printed and bound in Great Britain

CONTENTS

ACKNOWLEDGEMENTS

I am very grateful to the Springfield Project team for all its help and support in developing this work. It's a great team that is doing some really good work and I feel privileged to have been part of it. Also, a huge thank you to all the foster parents, adoptive parents, teachers, colleagues and friends who gave helpful feedback at various stages of the writing of this book and all the children who agreed to let me use their pictures. And last but not least, my family, for all their 'top tips', encouragement and support – thank you!

INTRODUCTION

I started writing this book when I was working in Fife, Scotland, between 2005 and 2013 as part of the Springfield Project, a joint Child and Adolescent Mental Health Service and Social Work team looking at the therapeutic needs of children who are in foster and adoptive care.

This book is about sensory integration, one of the therapies that we found to be helpful for these children. Developed originally by Dr A Jean Ayres, an Occupational Therapist, it offers a way of understanding how early movement experiences affect brain development.

We found that some children who had missed out on early movement experiences weren't able to do the more complicated things as they got older – like recognize how they're feeling on the inside.

We noticed a group of children who were so out of tune with themselves that they really struggled to manage to think about any sorts of feelings – even things like if they felt hot or cold or whether they could make their hearts beat faster by running around. Foster carers often talked about children seeming to have no sense of whether they felt hungry or full and described having to stop the children eating when they judged that they'd had enough, otherwise they would keep on eating until they made themselves sick. While some of that may be about an emotional emptiness, the more we heard about it and the more we worked with these children, the more we realized that there was also a physical component to it – they were dysregulated to the extent that they literally couldn't register how they felt on the inside. We realized that we needed to do something to address this before these children would be able to use psychological therapies to explore the emotional impact of their experiences.

While there are lots of good books around about sensory processing and sensory integration, we found that, because of the trauma these children had experienced, we couldn't just give teachers or parents activity ideas to do with children and let them get on with it.

These children's early experiences mean that they react to things in different ways to other children. So while crawling through a tunnel into a snug den might be a fun adventure for one child, it might remind another of being trapped and unable to get away from someone who was hurting them.

We realized that we needed to do something to address this dysregulation before these children would be able to use psychological therapies to explore the emotional impact of their experiences. By combining sensory integration theory and a neurosequential understanding of trauma, we were able to understand the importance of movement in forming a 'foundation layer' for social and emotional development.

While carrying out the work, we saw that good bodily awareness and functioning was really like the bottom layer of a tower of building blocks – the stable base that allows the rest of the tower to be built on top of it. We found that by understanding which systems were not adequately primed (i.e. hadn't had enough stimulation to get them into good working order), we were able to develop games and activities that let parents and children go back and fill in some of those gaps. By doing so, children became much more aware of themselves and their bodies – one teacher described the change as a child 'seeming much more comfortable in their own skin'. Following this, we noticed that children were much more able to regulate themselves – they stopped going too fast all the time and became able to stop and think sometimes. This leap in development made a huge difference to their everyday lives and gave us a platform to be able to help build relationships and learning.

This book is written for all those who are living and working with children who have been affected by early abuse and neglect. This will primarily be foster and adoptive parents, but social workers, adoption staff, teachers and others who play an important part in the child's life will also be able to use the ideas and suggestions in the book in their own setting. I have tried to bring together the relevant parts of sensory integration theory, clinical experience and research about how children process trauma and the impact this has on their sense of self and developing relationships.

While the book is informed by research and theory, you'll see as you read through that I haven't filled the book with references. Instead, I have provided a list of books and websites that will be useful sources of information if you wish to learn more about sensory integration and children who have experienced abuse or neglect.

I should also add that the emphasis of this book is on the *patterns of movement* that children have missed out on in their development and how they can be helped to go back and build them. It's not a book about the huge psychological impact of these early experiences on the child and their development – there are some excellent books already published on this, and I've listed some key titles in the recommended reading section.

I hope you find this book useful and that it will offer helpful insights and ideas to help you and your child.

PART ONE

INTRODUCING SENSORY INTEGRATION

The significance of early movement experiences

The brain and central nervous system are at the centre of everything that makes us human.

They work together to help us make sense of the world we live in and give us the tools to be able to relate, move, play, think, plan, anticipate and react. Attachment theory helps us understand the role of the early relationship in a child's developing sense of themselves and their world. It defines the kinds of experiences a baby and growing child needs to develop a robust sense of themselves and an idea of the world as a safe and reliable place. Babies and children growing up in loving, nurturing families have lots of movement and emotional experiences that generally allow their brains and central nervous systems to develop good, strong pathways that mean the child is able to move easily from one stage of development to the next.

It's lovely to see a parent 'chatting' to a small baby, and we usually notice their eye contact and the back and forth of their 'conversation' – how in tune they seem with each other. What we often don't notice is just how much the baby is moving as part of that interaction – usually their arms and legs are moving and they're wriggling and jiggling around. These movements, coupled with the interaction, are really important in building pathways in the brain and central nervous system that form the foundation for the development of emotional and social skills. Giving a baby lots of cuddles doesn't just give a nice 'feel-good' moment; those cuddles actually build pathways within the brain that will allow the child to think before they act, as they get bigger – this is *impulse control.*

Children who have experienced abuse or neglect in their early lives miss out on both aspects of this. They don't have the lovely, warm interactions or all the movement experiences that go with them. While babies may protest for some time when they're left on their own, after a time they give up and go into a kind of despair.

In this state the baby hardly moves at all – a baby lying in a cot who has given up hope that someone will come may do some self-soothing sorts of movements, such as moving their head, but they won't be doing the big whole-arm, whole-leg, excited sort of movements that we see babies doing when they're being chatted to or during big conversations with their parent.

This book is about understanding why this is important and how going back and redoing some of the movement experiences that have been missed can be really helpful to these children.

While some children are able to settle well into their new families, clinical experience suggests that simply taking a child out of an abusive situation and putting them into a loving family doesn't always solve all the problems.

Some children are able to use their new families to make sense of their early experiences and can absorb the loving care and opportunities that they have in their new family. However, another group of children struggle to do this and seem to continue to react to situations as if they were in an abusive environment. They seem burdened by their experiences and are often too agitated to be able to make use of talking or play-based therapies. Even interventions designed around improving the relationship between the parent and the child can be too difficult for very dysregulated children – they find it too difficult to be in a room with a therapist and can be very hard to contain and manage in a way that allows any useful therapeutic work to take place. Therapy often has to stop because the child has destroyed the toys or hurt the therapist or themselves. These children really struggle in school too. A very experienced teacher friend of mine described her experience of teaching a traumatized, adopted boy as being like having a grenade with the pin already pulled out of it in the classroom. She described how completely different it is from children with behavioural difficulties and the challenges that these children present. Having seen her in the classroom and been inspired by her teaching style, I was interested to hear her talk of how difficult she found it and how uncomfortable it often left her feeling. She talked about the dilemmas for the teacher – being there primarily to educate, but not being able to do that without first taking care of the child's emotional needs. This has to be done without having the training that gives understanding of the impact of these children's experiences, or being privy to the quality of information about what's going on in the rest of their lives. It is hard therefore to have a feel for the dynamics of the placement, and how interactions with school might go.

We talked about how incredibly challenging this is, and how easy it for schools to fall into the trap of providing containment and nurture (usually by very intuitive and caring classroom assistants), often leaving the child isolated from their peers and without the specialist assessment and education that a teacher can provide. We talked about how stressful it is, with school staff absorbing and managing huge amounts of distress and dysregulation, but because it's an education and not a clinical setting, there's no supervision to help them understand and manage their reaction and response to the child. And that was before we started talking about how deskilling it is that all the normal strategies that teachers might use to set the culture and tone of a classroom get completely scuppered by children with such profound difficulties.

On a physical level, these children often have difficulties with *regulation*. They struggle to tune into the messages their body is giving them about how they're feeling or reacting and use this information to make decisions about what they're going to do. This may be seen in their behaviour if they are too loud or go too fast all the time, or they may not be as agile as other children of the same age and may be a bit clumsy – bumping into things a lot or sliding themselves along walls as they walk.

They will often struggle with things like using cutlery or handwriting.

However, when we look more closely we notice that it's not just their hands that don't work very well. Their arms and shoulders aren't as strong as we would expect them to be and they don't work as well *together* as they need to in order to be able to do things like write, use a knife and fork or hang from the monkey bars in the play park.

Sensory integration theory offers a way of understanding how the brain processes and stores experience on a physical and an emotional level. It helps us to understand the effects of trauma and neglect as well as the impact on the developing brain of missed experiences. Putting these alongside clinical experience and research on trauma and attachment is helpful in understanding how children's early movements and sensory experiences, coupled with their trauma experiences, affect their emotional development.

To do this, we have to look carefully at the sorts of things that typically occur during infancy and early childhood and understand how the brain is shaped by these. For example, babies who spend lots of time on their tummies when they're awake generally develop better head, shoulder and neck control earlier. Repeated experiences of lying on their tummies builds and strengthens the pathways between the muscles they need to use to hold that position on their tummies and the brain and central nervous system. If a child doesn't lie on their tummy, those connections and pathways aren't built in the same way.

Strong muscles in these areas are the foundations for the next stage of development – learning to roll over – and the next one – supporting your own weight on your hands and knees so that you can learn to crawl. Control literally develops from the head downwards.

Understanding this helps us to work out how to use movement to try and build some pathways within the brain that would normally be laid down early on in a child's life. Children who have experienced abuse and neglect have often not had these 'foundation experiences'. It is possible to look at how the child moves and acts in their day-to-day life and, putting this together with what we know of the child's early experiences, begin to think about how to go back and redo some of the most important early movement experiences that they may have missed out on. This can make a huge difference for children's physical, social, emotional development and their learning.

Which children is this book about?

Before we think about that, it's important to differentiate between children who have a diagnosed *sensory processing disorder* and the children whom this book is about. Here it's useful to use the analogy of a computer. Think of a computer as having three main parts – a keyboard, a hard drive and a printer. If I want to print a document, first I have to write it (keyboard) and then the hard drive has to communicate with the printer so that I can print it. The screen offers a view of what I've input, and might give some clue as to what stage of processing it the computer is at.

If we apply that analogy to a child who is kicking a football, we have to stretch it a bit, but the input (keyboard) would be built up of all of the early patterns of movement that the child has had as a baby and developing child as well as the movement they make now as they're standing in front of the football. The hard drive would use all of the data that those experiences had built up as well as the input about what was happening right now to plan how and where the child should stand, how much force the kick should have, which leg would do the kicking, and what direction the ball would go in. These messages would then be sent to muscles and joints to get the body into a good position to kick the ball. The kicking of the ball would be the final stage – like the printing of the document.

For children who have sensory processing disorder, there can be difficulties at all stages of this – but they are usually in the processing of the information and the execution of the movements. Kranowitz (2005) outlines the current thinking in sensory integration theory (quoting the work of Miller et al.) and describes the way sensory processing disorder gets divided down into different categories with further subdivisions. I don't think that we need to go into the detail of that here, because the children we're considering are 'keyboard children', who haven't had the repeated patterns of movement as a baby and developing child. Their hard drive doesn't have enough information to work with and that's where we're going to begin –

inputting those movement experiences that have been missed. Thinking of the task we've asked the computer to do, namely, print a document – using this analogy it would be a bit like expecting it to be able to do that without having installed your Word programme.

That doesn't mean that a child who's suffered early trauma can't have a sensory processing disorder, but it's sensible to start by trying to redress the balance of not having had enough movement experiences within the context of those early attachment experiences (installing the programme and typing something in) before considering there might be something wrong with the hard drive or printer.

Before you go any further, it might be worth taking a few minutes to think about your child. If you've got more than one child, try and think of them one at a time. Jot down your thoughts in these bubbles:

How does your child move about?

Do they stand tall and seem quite muscular or are they more squirmy?

Can they manage to carry a glass of water in their hand while they walk along?

Do they have to hold it close to their body?

How do they manage things like holding a pencil or using cutlery?

How do they sit while they're watching TV or at their school desk?

Do they sit on their bottom or knees, lie on their tummies, hang upside down off the sofa or jump about?

Is there anything else you notice about the way your child moves or holds him or herself?

Do they like climbing and jumping or do they seem nervous when their feet leave the ground?

How do they manage on a trampoline?

Forming foundations

There's some quite obscure language in sensory integration theory but try not to get intimidated or bogged down by it – essentially the theory is a useful way of understanding how the brain develops and how repeated patterns of movement shape its development. It is often called a 'bottom-up' approach, describing the development of the systems of the brain and central nervous system in a sequential way, a bit like a tower made of blocks with one layer building on the next:

> This level is the higher-order things: problem solving, creative and logical thinking, managing feelings.

> Within this level is an awareness of different feelings, an ability to make sense of those feelings and an ability to make any changes needed for a task

> On this bottom level are basic physiological things like being able to recognize the difference between feeling tense and relaxed, hot and cold or when your tummy is full and when it is empty.

While it doesn't always happen in such a linear way in real life, it can be a helpful model because it explains how those early relationship experiences combined with bodily and movement experiences form the foundations for the development of social and emotional skills and learning. It allows us to look at what a child is struggling with but also what sorts of underlying skills a child would need to have to be able to perform at that level.

Throughout this book I'll make reference to Connor and Zoe (not real children, but amalgams of lots of children I've worked with) as we try to make sense of the different systems within sensory integration theory. But to start with, let me just introduce them.

Connor – peeling back the layers

Connor is an eight-year-old boy who is having lots of angry outbursts. When using this kind of model with children who have experienced early abuse and neglect, it is really important to hold on to the idea that development is fundamentally a sequential process. So, rather than going straight into something like anger management, it's helpful to think about the layers below managing feelings to see if Connor has mastered more basic bodily awareness and control – the bottom layer of the blocks. This means finding out if he is able to tune into himself on a bodily level – can he slow himself down or speed himself up to do everyday tasks like getting dressed or sitting down to colour in? Can he tell when he's hot or cold? Does he go out on a snowy day in a t-shirt and not notice that he's shivering and his skin feels cold? Is he able to tell when he's had enough to eat or does he keep on eating until he's likely to be sick? Does he actually taste the food or does he just launch it into the back of his mouth and swallow? Would he be able to think of a time he's felt tense or relaxed? Can he calm his body down?

We quickly discovered that Connor wasn't able to do any of these basic physiological things, so there really wasn't much point in trying to work on feelings – it would be a bit like trying to put the roof on a house without having built the walls. The work needs to start with the basic bodily sensations before moving on to those higher functioning things like feelings if our work with Connor and his adoptive family is going to have any chance of success.

Zoe – why is it important to think about what's been missed?

Zoe is a six-year-old child who was removed from her family home four years ago because of neglect, parental alcohol misuse and domestic violence. As a baby she had very little adult contact and few toys or company to amuse or comfort herself. Sometimes the TV was on but she was usually left on her own. Thinking about this on a purely physical level (we'll come back to Zoe and think about the emotional side of things later), it's helpful to consider the huge range of movement experiences that Zoe has missed out on that would be have been allowing her brain and central nervous system to build those foundation layers.

Zoe didn't go through the early movement experiences that would have let her progress through learning to roll over, sit up, crawl, pull herself up on things and then eventually walk. By the time she came into foster care at the age of four she was walking, but when we looked more closely we could see the effects of those gaps in her foundation experiences.

Not having had any of these early movement experiences – she was usually left lying in a cot or sitting in a baby seat – has left Zoe with real problems in getting her body to do what she wants it to. When she carries a cup of water she has to rest it on her chin to balance it otherwise all the water spills out as she walks. When she's sitting at the table drawing she has to concentrate quite hard on just sitting – something that most children can do without thinking. If she forgets to think about sitting and concentrates too much on her drawing or reaching for another pen she falls off her chair. Zoe is at school and the pressure is on to sit and write, to be able to get herself dressed for PE and to join in with the other children on the outdoor equipment at play time. She's trying to do complex, co-ordinated patterns of movement without having the foundation movement experiences that would have built the good head, neck and shoulder control that is essential for being able to go on and develop skills in doing much finer activities like handwriting.

Summary

I'll end this section with a summing up of the most important ideas.

- The brain and central nervous system are shaped by experiences.

- Each stage of development builds on the last one – learning, social and emotional development have to be built on a foundation of bodily awareness and control that comes from a rich variety of movement and sensory experiences. These begin while the baby is still in the womb and continue once the baby has been born.

- Bodily control is a top-down process – babies get control of their heads and necks first and this control moves down through the shoulders, arms, hands, body and finally the legs and feet. (You'll recognize this if you think of a baby sitting in a high chair eating finger food – babies are usually able to do this quite a long way before they can do something like walk or hop.)

- We can use this knowledge to help children who have been neglected. It does seem to be possible to go back and fill in the gaps left by missed experiences by taking children through certain patterns of movement. This is important in building a platform for 'higher level' functioning, like relationships, learning and the development of social and emotional skills.

- Children who have been neglected and abused have almost always had scary and upsetting experiences that have impacted on their brain development and how they process their experiences. It's much more complicated to help a child who has had experiences like this because you have to be constantly looking out for when they might 'startle' or suddenly shift into a different state of mind. While there are lots of ideas and suggestions in this book, the most important thing is to monitor really carefully the impact of any new movement experience on a child who has experienced maltreatment. This will come up a lot throughout the book, but it's an important caveat!

Parents, teachers and therapists can use the ideas and activities within this book to help most children who've been removed from home because they've been abused and neglected to progress. However, sometimes if a child is very dysregulated it can be hard to know where to start or what to do. Davie is an example of what this might look like.

_____Davie

Davie is five and when he gets stressed or overwhelmed his head and eyes start spinning round and he crashes and bangs about. It's quite alarming and almost looks as if his head might come right off his body. Now, to the untrained eye this might look like sensory seeking behaviour – as if he's trying to get enough input to get his body and brain into a position of being able to function well, but this might not be the case. He might be a child who is so hyperaroused that no amount of sensory input is going to be calming or help to get him into a good zone for learning. The sort of self-help approach that is talked about in this book is not for children whose difficulties are as extreme as Davie's – they need to have robust assessment and an individually tailored treatment package. If your child is experiencing behaviour similar to Davie's, it's best to ask for some professional help – often specialist

Occupational Therapists working in Child and Adolescent Mental Health Services (CAMHS) or paediatrics may be able to help.

Remember ages and stages

It can sometimes be hard to hold in mind the ages and stages of development when typically developing children reach certain milestones. There's a huge margin of difference within typical development, and all children develop at different rates. But, generally, we think of a child starting to sit up with some support by 6 months and being happy to sit on the floor and play with toys between about 9 and 12 months. Standing often comes next – children of about 11 months will often be able to pull themselves up to standing using something like a sofa or someone's legs and may take those first, wide-based steps any time from about 12 months. Girls are often a bit before boys with walking, but as with all things, the normal range is wide!

PART TWO

A SENSORY INTEGRATION THEORY PRIMER

To understand sensory integration, we'll begin by looking at normal or 'typical' development – breaking down how different experiences (emotional and physical) build different parts of the brain and how these parts work together to form a well-functioning system.

We'll then be able to think about children who have been neglected and try and make sense of the difficulties that they're having in light of what we know about brain development and how different experiences shape the brain.

Most importantly, we'll think about how children who have had such awful early lives can be helped, and how the results achieved can be better if we are able to use what we know about how movement experiences influence emotional development. As I'll explain, there are some aspects of managing the aftermath of trauma that do need therapy and professional help, but foster or adoptive families, schools and other professionals can do a huge amount in helping a child to fill in some of the gaps in their movement experiences so that their brains and central nervous systems are in a much better state to manage relationships and feelings.

Children spend so much of their lives at home and in school compared with how much time they might spend going to therapy. Having a home- or school-based approach to helping them means that progress can be made so much faster – it's possible to integrate activities into everyday life in a way that means you could be doing little bits to build functioning in different areas many times in a day.

Let's start by looking at brain development through the lens of sensory integration theory. As with everything to do with the brain, there are parts of this that are quite complicated, but perhaps the most important thing to bear in mind as we go through it are:

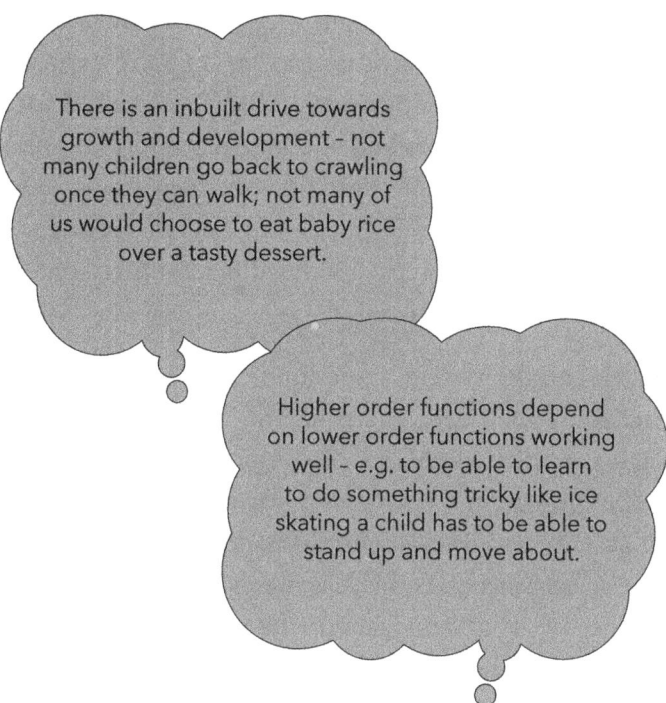

Relating this back to our layer of blocks, sensory integration theory would describe things using different terms and language:

Modulation and self-regulation

Auditory and visual systems

Vestibular, proprioceptive and tactile systems

Don't worry at this stage about what some of these words mean – apart from the visual system, we don't normally talk about proprioceptive or vestibular systems. What's really important to grasp is the idea that more complex skills build on a whole host of underlying skills. Bear in mind too that a well-functioning system needs good communication between all the different parts of the system.

There's another system – the limbic system – that goes through all the layers, and is like the music that's always playing in the background. We'll start by thinking about the limbic system – it's a useful way of looking at how a child's early trauma can continue to disturb and influence their development. It's this lens that will allow us to bring together what we know about the impact of trauma in children with how sensory integration can help. Some adoptive parents talk about seeing something in their child's eyes change, others notice their child becoming more giddy or wired. Once we can begin to spot it happening, we can begin to start to shift things, and that's what we'll do when we come onto Part Three.

The limbic system

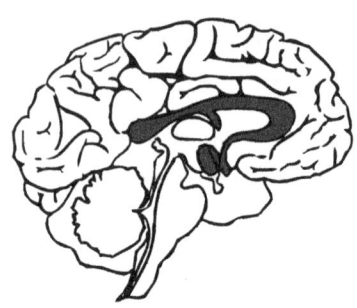

The limbic system is literally at the centre of your brain. If you make a fist with your hand and put your thumb underneath your fingers, imagine that the knuckles of your hand are your cerebral cortex (the higher functioning part of the brain for concentrating, problem solving, having ideas and controlling impulses), your wrist is your brainstem (which manages all the basic life systems like breathing, keeping you cool when you're hot or trying to warm you up when it's cold) and your thumb is the limbic system. Snuggled right in the middle of the brain, it has the huge job of linking the parts of the brain that are concerned with important physiological functions like heart rate, breathing and digestion (the brainstem) with the higher functioning areas (the cerebral cortex).

The limbic system works largely outside conscious awareness. When it's working well, it allows you to gauge your response to a situation and work out your reaction. But all of this depends on earlier experiences and the way that memories and experiences are stored. This is where all those early nurturing and movement experiences are so important, and why we need to think so carefully about them for children who have experienced neglect and maltreatment.

Before we can think about that, we need to know about three main players in the limbic system – the *amygdala*, the *hippocampus* and the *hypothalamus* – and what a well-functioning limbic system looks like. We'll think about them each separately first, but it's important to remember that there are lines of communication working between all the parts of the system all the time. Again this is a bit technical (and it's always difficult to understand things that operate outside our conscious awareness) but hopefully you'll be able to see how helpful it is to be able to understand it.

Amygdala

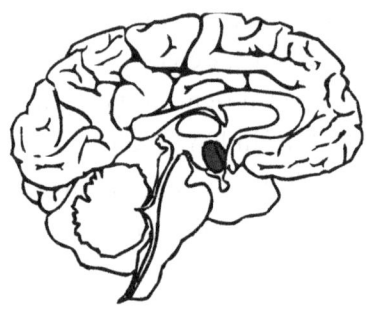

The *amygdala* (named after the Greek word for almond, which perfectly describes its shape) plays a really important role in processing emotions (working out whether a situation is scary, pleasant, exciting, boring, etc.) and linking with the higher functioning parts of the brain (cerebral cortex) and the parts of the brain that prepare the body for immediate action (brainstem). This idea of 'what sort of emotional experience is it?' is key in the brain deciding how to react. How the brain decides on the type of experience usually depends on our past experiences. In a typically developing child, the early mother–baby interactions (feeding, cuddles, being carried around in a baby sling, 'chatting', singing and generally all the warm parent–infant interactions) coupled with repeated patterns of movement help the baby's brain to develop really strong links between the amygdala and the frontal lobe (which is at the front of the cerebral cortex).

Think of a very small baby lying on a mat while their mother sings and chats to them. The baby isn't still for a moment – it's moving its arms, feet, mouth and head). Now you might wonder why this is so important, but it's these connections between the amygdala and the frontal lobe that will allow the developing child to stop and think about how they're feeling. This is crucial – without a window of thinking between impulse and action the child is reacting to things without being able to first think about and plan their reaction. On a practical level first – imagine a child who's walking to the park to play football. They're carrying their ball under their arm, but suddenly they drop it and it rolls across the road. Their impulse is to get their ball, but unless they've developed the capacity to think, they're likely to run straight out into the road and perhaps get hit by a car. Good connections between the amygdala and the frontal lobe allow the child to do that vital piece of thinking – 'I want my ball but I'd better check if any cars are coming before I run into the road'. In a different situation, being able to tune into and recognize if the feeling in your tummy is anger or excitement gives you good information that helps to plan how you're going to respond to any given situation. Imagine how confusing life would be if you were only aware of a swirling in your tummy and had no idea what it meant.

Hypothalamus

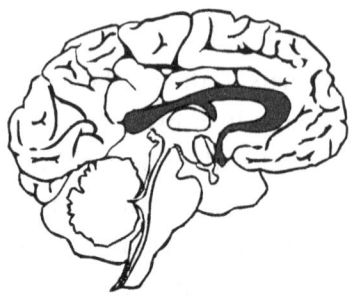

The next important part of the limbic system is the *hypothalamus*. This is a tiny structure but it has a massive job to do, particularly in managing stress. The hypothalamus controls the autonomic nervous system, a system that works outside our conscious awareness. There are two 'arms' to the autonomic nervous system, the sympathetic nervous system and the parasympathetic nervous system. The sympathetic nervous system is concerned with 'fight or flight' reactions (that rush of adrenalin and energy that allows us to run away from something chasing us or turn and shout at someone who's threatening us), and the parasympathetic nervous system with keeping things calm and at a level of arousal that is best suited to being able to take in and think about what's going on around us.

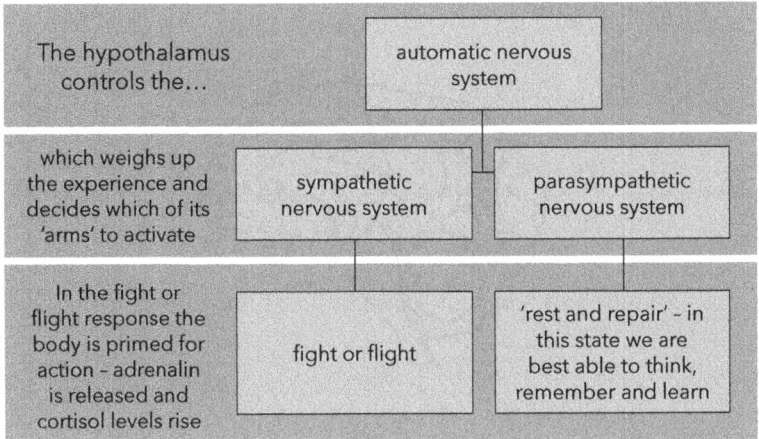

The hypothalamus has lots of connections with the *endocrine system*, which, among other things, triggers the release of the stress hormone cortisol. In clinical settings, we often see children whose level of arousal is much too high for the situation they're in, and in these cases it's often that their bodies are still reacting to situations as if they're dangerous and threatening rather than weighing up the current situation.

Hippocampus

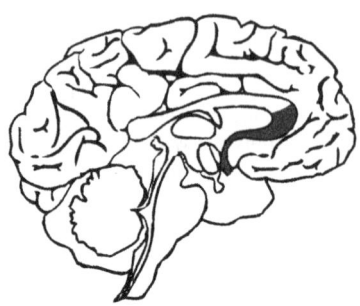

The *hippocampus* communicates with the endocrine system to switch off the stress hormone cortisol. The hippocampus is also really important in the making of memories. Studies of people who have experienced trauma show that they have much smaller hippocampi than other people. Another study showed that London taxi drivers have much bigger hippocampi.

Understanding how the hippocampus works and how it links in with all the other systems in the limbic system will help us know how to help traumatized children build pathways that will allow them to store new, good experiences. Let's try and think about how an experience is processed:

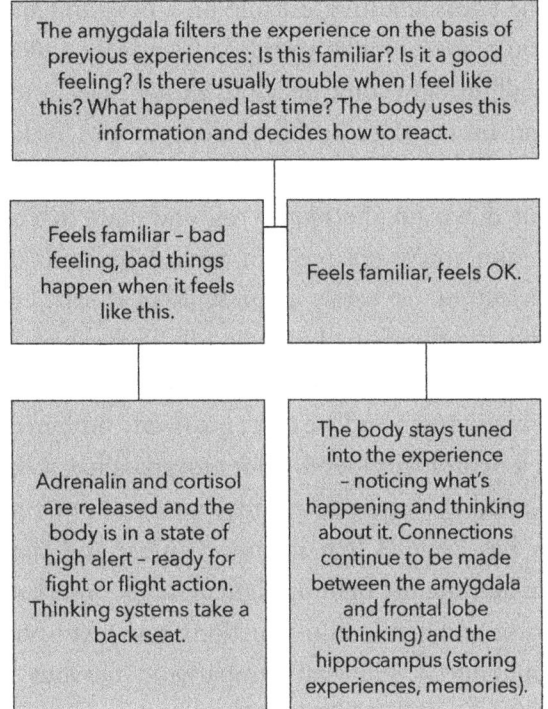

The amygdala filters the experience on the basis of previous experiences: Is this familiar? Is it a good feeling? Is there usually trouble when I feel like this? What happened last time? The body uses this information and decides how to react.

Feels familiar - bad feeling, bad things happen when it feels like this.

Feels familiar, feels OK.

Adrenalin and cortisol are released and the body is in a state of high alert - ready for fight or flight action. Thinking systems take a back seat.

The body stays tuned into the experience - noticing what's happening and thinking about it. Connections continue to be made between the amygdala and frontal lobe (thinking) and the hippocampus (storing experiences, memories).

As you can see, when something galvanizes the sympathetic nervous system response (fight or flight) then the parts of our brain that help develop thinking about how we feel and storing new memories are completely out of the loop. It's helpful to bear this in mind – it can explain a lot about how children from abusive families can be in a kind and loving family and yet still react as if they're in danger. Another way to understand how the autonomic nervous system works is by thinking about an everyday situation.

Imagine yourself sitting outside on a beautiful summer's day. You've met some of your best friends for a picnic and you've all brought some delicious things to eat and drink. You can hear a river burbling along in the background and feel the warmth of the sun on your face. You settle yourself down on the picnic rug and start to chat to a friend who you've not seen for ages. A fly lands on your arm. Most of us barely even register the fly, perhaps noticing it enough to brush it off. We've had enough experience of flies landing on us to know that they don't cause us any harm and we don't get overly bothered about it. On a neurological level, your amygdala has recognized and filtered the experience and your autonomic nervous system has decided that it's not a threat and there's no need to activate the fight or flight systems. Your heart rate stays nice and stable and you don't start over-breathing or panicking – your parasympathetic nervous system is keeping everything in that 'just right' zone and you can carry on chatting with your friends and having a nice lunch.

Now imagine yourself in that same situation but now the picnic is just four weeks after you had a bad bee sting in your garden. You had a really bad reaction to the sting and had to go into hospital for life-saving treatment. It's taken you ages to feel better again and you've not ventured back out into your garden since it happened. How do you think you feel this time round? Your body responds completely differently – at the first sign of a flying, buzzing creature the amygdala recognizes and remembers danger. The sympathetic nervous system leaps into action and triggers a host of bodily responses – including increased heart rate and blood pressure – and dampens down others – like digestion and the sort of easy relaxed mood you've been in that's allowed you to chat and enjoy your friends' company. The body is in a state of heightened arousal and ready to do whatever it has to do to respond to the threat. By the time you realized it's only a fly that's landed on your arm you're already primed for fight or flight and your parasympathetic nervous system has to take over, slowing your heart rate down, letting your blood pressure drop and trying to get your body to go back to its unstressed state. And that's just one bee. Now imagine that you'd been attacked by swarms of bees two or three times a day for four months. You wouldn't calm down nearly as fast, would you? Your system would stay aroused and alert, knowing that danger is always around the corner. We know that memories associated with fear last a long time. Now imagine that instead of it being an adult and swarming bees, it is a child and abuse and neglect that's happened day in, day out, for most of their lives, and we can begin to see why their 'off' switch doesn't kick in.

If we think of children who have had months and perhaps years of abuse and neglect, we can begin to understand the importance of trying to get the child into a state of mind where they feel safe and happy before we try to do anything that we're hoping they'll be able to remember or fall back on another time.

Thinking about it in terms of the limbic system, these children are functioning all the time on their sympathetic nervous systems – their levels of arousal are much too high and this inhibits the development of pathways in the brain that are about storing good memories and getting back to a less aroused state, emotionally and physically. Understanding the sympathetic and parasympathetic nervous systems is key to being able to change this.

Some people have described it as being a bit like an emotional short-circuiting – it's as if children who have experienced a lot of maltreatment and neglect have systems that short-circuit the normal processes and shoot straight to the sympathetic arm of the autonomic nervous system – fight or flight – hyperarousal.

Other people have described it as being like living with an over-sensitive smoke alarm inside your head. It would be a bit like the smoke alarm going off when you go to fill the kettle or put the stove on – the merest sniff of something that might be in the vicinity of something that might once have been dangerous is enough to set the smoke alarm ringing. This triggers the fight or flight response without the child being able to stop and notice what's going on around them and think about whether it really is a dangerous situation. Imagine trying to go out every day of your life with a smoke alarm that rings in your head as often as that.

The example of the bees was a very simple one, where it's quite easy to see the connection between a scary event and a reaction. Unfortunately, it's not always that straightforward. Our experiences build up our perception of the world, layer by layer over time, until the foundation layers are so long ago that we can't recall them; it's often impossible to trace the thread that goes from reaction to foundation experience. You might recognize this when you think about meeting people that you either 'click' with or take an instant dislike to. Sometimes, if we think about this, we can see how this new person might remind of us a person we used to know, but other times it's hard to make sense of it. Children who have experienced abuse and neglect usually can't explain why they've done something or reacted in a certain way. It's not usually that they're being deliberately obstructive, but the underlying reasons will be buried deep and they probably won't have access to them.

It's important to be able to notice when your child has shifted into a fight or flight response, because the first job is to try and get them back into the state of mind where they're feeling safe and calm.

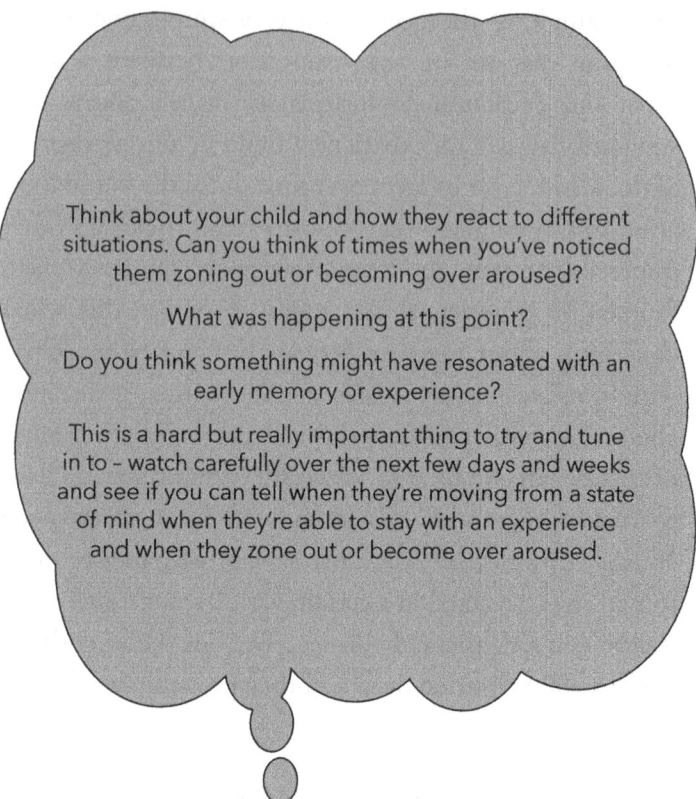

Think about your child and how they react to different situations. Can you think of times when you've noticed them zoning out or becoming over aroused?

What was happening at this point?

Do you think something might have resonated with an early memory or experience?

This is a hard but really important thing to try and tune in to - watch carefully over the next few days and weeks and see if you can tell when they're moving from a state of mind when they're able to stay with an experience and when they zone out or become over aroused.

We'll move on now to think about the vestibular, proprioceptive and tactile systems. Keep in mind the limbic system, think of it as the music that's always playing in the background.

The vestibular system

It's our vestibular system that helps us to balance and allows us to right ourselves when we start to fall. It helps our eyes to keep looking straight ahead even if we're driving over bumpy ground and gives us a sense of security and connectedness with the earth.

It plays a really important role in getting us ready for fight or flight in an emergency. If a child has a poorly developed or a poorly regulated vestibular system, they may have problems with what is called postural control – this affects things like balance and orientation. It's sometimes helpful to think of the body as being a bit like a mechanical crane, with the trunk as the main body of the crane and arms and legs as the arm of a crane. To be able to pick up heavy loads or place things precisely, the crane has to be well secured – a crane that's not well grounded or with a body that isn't strong enough isn't going to be safe or effective. It's the same with our bodies – unless we have a good stable base from our head and shoulders down to our pelvis, any sort of arm or leg movement is likely to be a bit precarious. You might have noticed some children who hold themselves very rigidly when they're trying to do something – these are often children with poor postural control. They may find things like standing still with their eyes closed really difficult (because they can't use their other senses like vision to keep themselves balanced) and they topple over.

The vestibular system forms the foundation for all the other sensory systems, so it's really important that we first pay attention to how it develops. Like all the sensory systems, the vestibular system needs to be 'fed' lots of movement experiences. The receptors for the vestibular system which receive information about head movement and gravity are located in the ears and these link to the brain and central nervous systems, like wires carrying information back and forward between the body and the brain and central nervous system. These receptors are activated by head movements (we're getting very technical now) – within the ear there are receptors called *otoliths* that detect linear movement (movement in a straight line like swinging on a swing) while *ampulla* in the semi-circular canals of the inner ear detect rotatory movements (like going round on a roundabout). To have a well-functioning vestibular system, the developing child needs lots of experiences of head movement to stimulate and feed these receptors.

Thinking about a baby, let's try and imagine how these different parts of the vestibular system get stimulated. First of all the *otoliths* – remember that these detect linear movement. They are working all the time in response to gravity. Think about a baby lying in a cot or pram. What causes their head to move? They might turn their head to look at a mobile – stimulating the otoliths, or turn their head to the sound of their mother's voice – again the otoliths. Interesting things in the environment make them turn to look and once their interest has been captured they might stay and enjoy it for a while.

Think of what we might do to try and comfort a crying baby. We might rock them gently in our arms or hold them close to us and sway a bit from side to side to try and calm them down. These sorts of movements are also very stimulating for the otolith parts of the vestibular system.

The earliest sort of stimulation for the ampulla in the semi-circular canals is the last couple of months in the womb when the baby is upside down and moving around. Once a baby is out in the world, all the effort involved in learning to get control of their head is very stimulating for this system – along with things like learning to roll over. (Think about the sequential part – babies who have spent time on their tummies will be in a much better state to do things like rolling over – not only will they have the strength to do it but they'll also have the confidence to explore, as they have not spent the last few months only looking at the ceiling or straight ahead!)

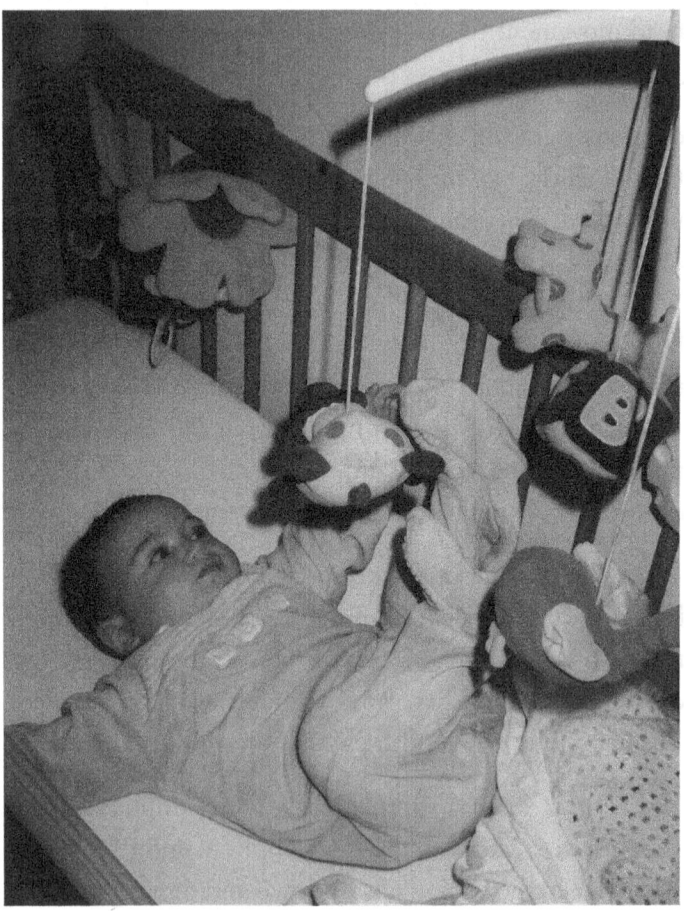

Even carrying a baby around on your hip while you're busy doing things involves a lot of moves and changes of direction and can be very stimulating to the vestibular system. As the baby moves into toddlerhood, rough and tumble play, where there is lots of chasing and changes of direction continues to stimulate the vestibular system. If you watch primary school age children playing you'll see lots of games and activities that continue to be very stimulating for the vestibular system – playing roly poly, hanging upside down from bars, doing handstands and cartwheels, spinning around, and going round and round on roundabouts. Just watching the play of typically developing children gives lots of information about how these systems are fed and develop throughout the child's early years.

Under-activated vestibular systems

Lots of children who have been abused and neglected will have missed out on the sorts of early movement experiences needed to build a well-functioning vestibular system. In clinical work, we see and hear of babies who have been left in their cots, hungry and unsoothed, for hours and sometimes days on end. Children who should be toddling around are often left strapped in car seats or chairs, perhaps with the TV on to keep them quiet. Setting aside the emotional impact of this for a moment, this lack of normal activity means that these children won't have the sorts of movement experiences needed to adequately prime the vestibular system. What we notice in children with poor vestibular functioning are things like:

Low muscle tone and poor posture - this really affects everything from being able to keep upright to things like getting dressed and kicking a ball.

Fearfulness about movement or very sensory seeking behaviour - crashing, banging and whizzing around. and never getting tired.

Poor balance and co-ordination - this makes things like scooting, writing, using scissors, catching a ball and playing a game of tig really difficult.

How does limited head movement as a baby lead to poor muscle tone, balance and co-ordination? Well, here's where it gets a bit more technical again but again stay with it because being able to grasp this will make it easier to understand why we're suggesting certain sorts of movement patterns for children with deficiencies in this system. Breaking things down into tiny steps is a good way to think about how to rebuild a more robust system.

Let's take the otoliths first (stimulated by linear movements – like being rocked as a baby). Once the otolith receptors have been activated, they send signals down the spine to the muscles that help us to lengthen out and stand straight – these muscles are in the head, neck, trunk and knees.

These repeated patterns of movement strengthen these muscles – think 'lengthen and strengthen' for the otolith part of the vestibular system. Being able to stand up tall and have a good strong core are the foundations for postural control and being able to keep our balance. A strong core means that we're able to stand up straight and aren't sagging in the middle.

A foster carer recently remarked to me that he'd noticed over the years that when he lifts up a looked-after child it's a completely different experience to lifting up a typically developing child. With a typically developing child there's usually a 'weightiness' about them – you get a feel for their muscularity – whereas looked-after children have a floppiness about them – a core that's like cooked spaghetti with no strength or feeling of being held together.

Stimulating the semi-circular canals (with rotatory head movements or movements of the head at different angles, such as a baby rolling over or a toddler playing roly-poly or being 'flown' around their dad's head) also sends signals to the brain and down the spinal cord. They go to the muscles of the head, neck and upper part of the trunk, contributing again to good postural control (especially head control). In addition, they're also involved in *occulomotor* functioning – the connection between your eyes and movement. An ice skater who can perform lots of twirls without getting dizzy is a good example of well-tuned occulomotor functioning – essentially it's what allows you to keep your balance when doing things while you're moving, like swinging on a swing or running across uneven ground. Your eyes keep having to adjust to keep your visual field still – if the landscape moved as much as your body it would be hard to stay upright!

So, all of these foundation blocks of balance, postural stability and oculomotor functioning fed by these very early head movements. If a child hasn't got a stable core – like the crane we thought about earlier – movements that involve their arms and legs are all going to be difficult.

Let's think for a moment about a child who hasn't. Remember Zoe who we first met on page 23?

Zoe – an example of poor vestibular and proprioceptive functioning

It's interesting to watch Zoe as she tries to sit at a desk and write. When she forgets to think about sitting and concentrates hard on trying to draw or write, she often falls off the chair.

This illustrates just how much she has to concentrate on each little aspect of her movement – her balance and movement systems are so underdeveloped that she can't just rely on her body to keep itself where she put it as most of us can, she really has to focus her attention on that. Once she has got into a stable sitting position (perhaps being held in place by cushions or a helpful adult), she locks her arm down by her side to try and get more control over her hands.

She has so little control of her arms and hands that she has to try and use the big muscles of her shoulder and trunk to keep her arm and hand still enough for her to be able to write. This is made more difficult by the fact that her legs keep swinging as she tries to write, so she's wobbling a lot which is making her even less stable.

In typical development, those repeated patterns of movement that allow a child to gain control over their body and movements, from head control to rolling over, learning to crawl, etc., allow the brain and muscles to work out which parts of the body are needed for which movements and how much force is needed. So typically, by the time children have got to Zoe's age, they have good control of the big movements of their bodies (especially the shoulder girdle if we're thinking about writing) and are getting better at fine movements. Fine motor skills are harder because they happen further away from the body (remember control happening closer to the body – in this case shoulder girdle and postural control) before children can do things like handwriting which is a smaller movement that happens further away from the body. Repeated patterns of movement during early development also help the body do something called specialisation. If you watch a baby having a 'conversation' with their mum, their arms and legs will probably be moving at the same time as their eyes and heads. As the child matures and, providing they have enough repeated patterns of movement, they begin to lose some of these superfluous movements. A toddler uses fewer whole body movements when having a conversation than the baby. In the same way the body prunes the extra movements that aren't helpful to an activity – in Zoe's case writing isn't helped by her swinging legs and it's fair to assume that if she'd not had such an abusive and deprived early life, her system would be much better primed and she'd be more able to sit still to write.

Her foster mum changing from sitting on the sofa when reading a story to rocking in slow repetitive movements in a rocking chair will not only feed the vestibular system, it will also help to grow useful pathways in the limbic system (see page 32) around attachment and nurturing. Swinging gently on a swing will also be really helpful to her, as well as doing lots of activities that involve lying on her tummy (remember the otoliths – lengthen and strengthen), for example at this stage, lying on the floor to do colouring in will be more helpful than trying to do it at the table.

It's trickier to do lots of rotatory movements because children can very easily become a bit sick and dizzy, especially if their system is very underdeveloped, so it's important to start off very slowly and really track how the child is managing. Short bursts of low-intensity movements are the best way to start. Slow, rhythmical, up-and-down or forward-and-back movements tend to be experienced as more comforting and grounding. Remember, for children with poor balance and postural control, whizzing round on a roundabout could be a really scary experience and make them quite sick.

Before going on to think about activities that would be helpful for children like Zoe, we need think about the proprioceptive and tactile systems, because together they form the bottom layer of our blocks of development.

The proprioceptive system

It's our proprioceptive system that allows us to pick up a cup of coffee and take it to our mouths to drink in a controlled way rather than throwing it over our shoulder or spilling it down our front, or give someone a hug without squeezing all the breath out of them. It's all about the smooth, co-ordinated working of muscle groups that extend (lengthen) and contract (shorten) the muscles. The registration of the information travelling through these muscle groups to the brain and back to the muscles helps to inform us of how to respond in relation to pressure, strength, etc. and helps us to work out how much force is required for a movement. Good proprioception is having a really good grasp of what your body is doing without having to look carefully at that part of your body. An adoptive mum talked about her child, saying that they'd been digging in the garden and he'd been concentrating really hard on what he was doing. She asked him if he'd like a drink and, taking his eyes off his fork for a moment, he said that he would. At the same time, he put the fork through his foot. When his mum looked shocked, he said that he hadn't known that was where his foot was. That's a good example of poor proprioceptive functioning – not really knowing where your body is unless you're looking at it.

Some examples of good proprioceptive functioning include:

Putting your hair up in a ponytail – you can't use your eyes to help your hands work out what to do).

Doing star jumps – both sides of the body need to move at the same time and with the same force.

Throwing a ball accurately – you have to be able to judge force and distance and adjust your throw accordingly.

Like the example with the boy in the garden, it's perhaps easier to describe the proprioceptive system by thinking of what we see when it isn't working well. Movements are often poorly modulated – either really jerky or really floppy. There is often a lot of overshooting with movements – for example throwing a ball much too hard and never quite seeming to be able to adjust the strength of the throw to get it right.

When doing handwriting at school, these children might either press so hard that their pencil goes right through the page or write so lightly that it's hard to read. Children with poor proprioceptive functioning are often described as tripping over fresh air – always bumping into things. They might be really fidgety (they have to do lots of movements to get enough proprioceptive feedback about where their body is and what the different parts are doing) or they might rush through their movements.

With the proprioceptive system, we don't need to go into the different pathways as much as we did with the vestibular system – it's really enough to know that a child needs a wide range of movement experiences to build a good proprioceptive system and to remember the order in which the developing child gains muscle control and strength. As you'll have noticed by now, sensory integration is all about hierarchies and small steps of development working towards a well-functioning system. So let's think about the proprioceptive system in that same way.

Think about the movement patterns a typically developing baby goes through as they progress through the different stages – from lying to rolling to crawling to walking. We've thought a bit about the strengthening of the shoulder girdle muscles that happens when babies are on their tummies and beginning to prop themselves up. We've also thought a bit about rolling over and its importance in building a good vestibular system. Now let's think about the baby getting ready to crawl. Before they actually 'take off' they often spend a lot of time on their hands and knees rocking back and forwards. This sends lots of messages through the muscles to the movement areas of the brain (proprioceptive feedback), teaching them where the muscles and joints are in relation to the rest of the body and testing out different movements.

It's the same when a child is learning to walk – there are all those weeks of them pulling themselves up on furniture or letting adults know that they really want to be on their feet and held in an upright position. Think of all the time parents spend bent over their child as they try to take their first steps. Before they step out they usually spend quite a lot of time just standing, then swaying and then perhaps lifting a foot up and putting it down. It's all these repeated patterns of movement that help the body build up a good map of the muscles and joints and learn about how much force and effort is needed.

The development of control happens from the head downwards – so babies get control of their head, neck and shoulder muscles first, then gradually get control of their trunk, their pelvic girdle and finally their legs and feet, as explained earlier. Unless there are some developmental problems, it's unusual to see babies who can walk before they can feed themselves or children who can write but who have no head control. It's all incremental, with one step building on the last.

Let's go back to our crane analogy (see page 45). If the vestibular system is like the body of the crane, the proprioceptive system is like the arm. The vestibular system provides a stable base that allows the crane to do all sorts of lifting, moving and positioning. It's just the same in the developing child – good postural control and balance (the vestibular system) form a solid foundation for the development of movement (the proprioceptive system). We need to remember that movements that happen close to the body (like shoulder movements) will be more stable than those that happen further away (like writing, trying to tie shoelaces, hopping, skipping or tap dancing) and that children will first become confident with movements closest to the trunk and then get better at those that are further away.

Under-activated proprioceptive systems

What we see in children with under-activated proprioceptive systems is movements that are poorly modulated:

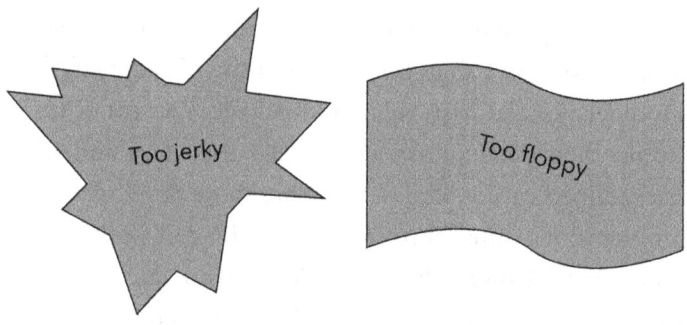

The tactile system

The *tactile system* forms the last component of our building blocks and is probably the easiest to understand. On a functional level, it's almost completely intertwined with the *proprioceptive system*. In books about sensory integration they are often grouped together and called the *somatosensory system*.

The proprioceptive system is concerned with sensations and feedback from within the body (joints and muscles) while the tactile system is concerned with sensations from outside the body – touch in all its forms. Touch receptors are located all over the body – there's a great illustration of this called the homunculus – it's worth Googling to have a look at it. Some areas of our body have far more receptors than others. Think about your own body – most of us are far more sensitive to touch on our faces than, for example, our elbows. Different receptors have different functions – detecting pain or temperature or discriminating between shapes or textures.

It's helpful to separate the tactile system from the other systems when thinking about children who have missed out on a lot of experiences, because, as we'll see, it can be a useful starting point for rebuilding underdeveloped systems.

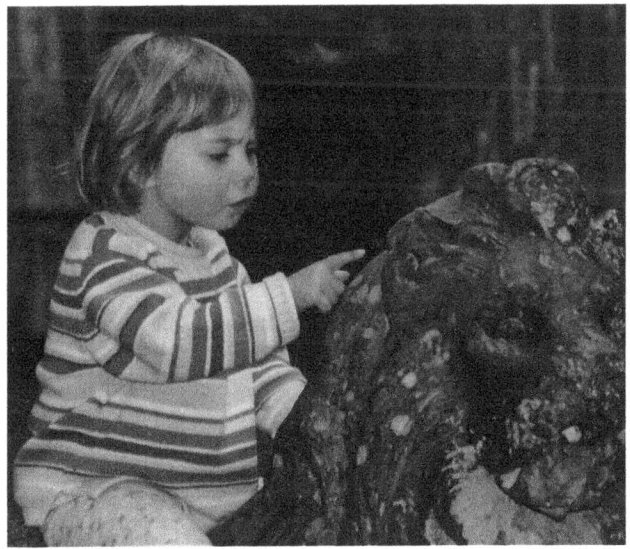

Touch is vital in the developing child's growing awareness and mastery of their surroundings.

Being able to explore and recognize objects through touch is closely linked with visual skills. Different kinds of touch receptors are located all over our bodies and in our mouths. Some are protective and register pain or pleasure, while others are what's called 'discriminative' – they help us to explore and recognize objects throughtouch.

As with the vestibular and proprioceptive systems, all this information is carried back to the central nervous system where it is processed and stored. This builds a map of our world that is used as reference for future experiences.

For typically developing children whose parents meet their physical and psychological needs well enough most of the time, the tactile system evolves from being mainly a protective system (in infancy) to being mainly a discriminatory one that allows for much greater exploration of their environment. The shift is really from survive to thrive.

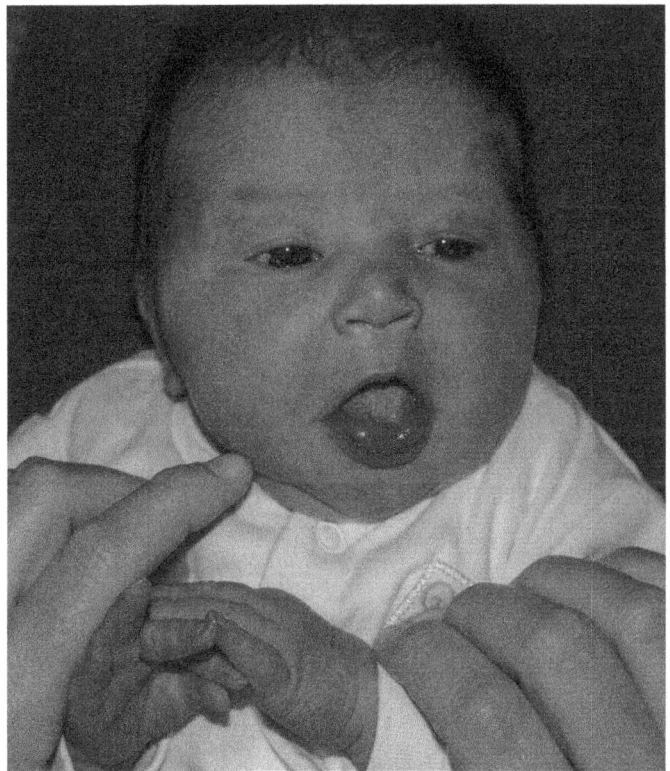

Infancy

In infancy, survival is paramount and the whole system is primed for that. What the baby experiences over its first weeks and months will determine the extent to which their system is able to evolve from this point.

Toddlers

If toddlers have had enough good experiences of being safe as babies, and touch in all its forms (e.g. feeding, dressing) was nurturing and comforting, their system will still be primed for survival but it will be evolving to allow for more exploration.

Into childhood

As the child develops and they continue to experience the world as a safe and reliable place, the protective arm of the tactile system can fade and exploration can begin in earnest!

Summary

Sensory integration's description of the limbic, vestibular, proprioceptive, and tactile systems offers a way of understanding how the brain and body process experiences on a physical as well as an emotional level. As we have seen, development of bodily control and emotional competence are sequential processes, with each new layer building on the one before. When considering a child's emotional difficulties where there has been early neglect or abuse, it can be helpful to think about these other systems and whether the child is trying to build complex social and emotional skills on a firm foundation of good bodily awareness and sensory processing.

PART THREE

APPLYING OUR KNOWLEDGE OF SENSORY INTEGRATION

There are really good sensory integration books that offer ideas for children with sensory processing disorders, but, as we've seen, the problem for children who have experienced abuse and neglect is more about a lack of sensory input than a processing disorder. Remember the computer analogy? These are the 'keyboard children', who have lacked the movement experiences that go alongside typically developing attachment relationships in the early days and the movement and exploration that a child in a stimulating and loving environment experiences – reaching for a toy, crawling towards a sibling, etc. Children who have experienced abuse and neglect have usually had a dearth of input. So they have significant gaps in their early movement experiences and at the same time they've had lots of neglectful, abusive experiences that have wired their brains up in a really unhelpful way. In this section I'll explain how using the principles of sensory integration can help to redress this balance. Understanding which of the child's systems are most underdeveloped and then using games and activities designed to take the child back through movements and experiences that have been missed develops much better bodily awareness and control. This helps children tune into themselves on a bodily level – recognising the difference between feeling stressed and relaxed or hot and cold – as well as helping to develop greater adeptness in tasks requiring co-ordination and dexterity, like riding a bike or sitting still to do handwriting at school.

All of this in turn builds a good, stable platform for the development of social and emotional skills, which are important for learning. What sensory integration and an understanding of trauma teaches us is that these skills have to be built on a foundation of good bodily awareness and functioning. But the challenge is huge! It's very important to do things in small steps, making sure the child is both competent and confident on one step before moving to the next one.

Where to start

A sensible place to start trying to recalibrate the limbic system is by using the tactile system. Remember the evolution of the tactile system? It moves from being mainly protective in infancy to being primed for exploration and discovery. This is helpful because it's very similar to what we're trying to do with the limbic system: to shift it from being in high alert to allowing the child to stay in the moment of an experience and think about and understand what's happening. From what we know about the limbic system, when children are in a hyperaroused state (remember the fight or flight arm of the sympathetic nervous system), they are less able to take in and process information or experiences in a way that allows them to make new memories. We need to work out how to strengthen the parasympathetic arm of their autonomic nervous system so that they can lower their arousal levels and begin to build memories and learn other ways of managing day-to-day life. We need to recalibrate that constant vigilance and watchfulness so that they can start taking in information from the here and now rather than the past. We want them to be able to stay in the moment of an experience and hold on to and remember it in a way that means it's helpful to them.

Games and activities that help to shift the child's tactile system from being on high alert/protective functioning to being primed for exploration work well. By starting with relatively simple tasks, and with just you and your child together, it should be possible to work out whether your child is functioning in a fight or flight/high alert mode, or whether they're shifting to a state of mind that they're able to stay in the moment and absorb, make use of and store the experiences that they're having.

This is where we started with Connor.

Building tactile functioning

———— Connor - rebuilding early foundations

When Connor came into foster care, his foster mum was impressed by his hearty appetite and how unfussy he seemed. It was only when she looked a bit more carefully at this that she realized that he wasn't actually tasting anything that he was putting in his mouth, but was really just throwing food to the back of his mouth and swallowing. He didn't seem to be able to register when he was full and she felt that if she didn't stop him he would keep on eating until he was sick.

We began our work with Connor and his foster mum by focusing on this area. His early experiences meant that feeding hadn't been a comforting, nourishing time, and he had learned to grab what he could eat when he could, never quite knowing were the next meal was coming from. In our sessions we tried to build some associations between food and 'mouthly' activities and pleasure in the hope that he might be able to begin to slow down enough to build his awareness of his bodily sensations, learning to both taste what he was eating and notice how full he was feeling.

Most children enjoy doing a 'taste test' of trying to guess which flavour crisps are which in a blind test, and Connor was no exception. Like many children who have had upsetting early feeding and care experiences, Connor really struggled to hold the crisps in his mouth for long enough to taste them, so we had to take things really slowly.

We began with just two flavours– salt and vinegar and smoky bacon – both of which are quite strong and distinctive. Mum would show Connor the packet so that he'd know which flavours he was tasting (to take away any anxiety) and then she'd put them into two different bowls and he'd try and guess which was which.

When he got good at that, she would put the crisps into three bowls – two had the same flavour and one had a different flavour – and Connor had to try and guess which two were the same.

The next step was to introduce more flavours one at a time until Connor was able to taste a range of different flavours and tell which was which.

By this time Connor was really enjoying the taste tests and his mum was able to branch out and try other things – such as trying to tell the difference between jam, chocolate spread and peanut butter, knowing whether he was eating a pea or a piece of sweet corn or thinking about how a raspberry tasted different to a strawberry.

As well as tasting games, some of the 'mouthly activities' that worked well included:

» Using an electric toothbrush to play 'mouthly' games - brushing his teeth and gums and getting used to the pleasant sensation in his lips and tongue. The primary purpose of this activity wasn't to clean his teeth but to increase the amount of pleasant sensory stimulation he got to his mouth and gums.

» Playing blowing games – blow football (with a ping pong ball and a straw), blowing bubbles and putting two cm of milk into a tall glass and seeing if he could blow enough bubbles to get the milk right to the top of the glass. Connor really liked this one, and we were able to grade it by starting with quite a big straw and then moving to straws with smaller and smaller diameters.

» Trying food that gives lots of sensory stimulation – like popping candy, grapes that have been frozen, sherbet or carrot sticks.

» Drinking very thick milkshake/fruit smoothie drinks with a very small straw to really increase sensory feedback and effort.

These activities also help with oral motor development and low muscle tone around the mouth, which is useful for children who have been abused and neglected and who dribble a lot or have speech and language delay.

We did this alongside lots of other activities designed to build Connor's ability to tune into his body and notice what his body was doing. Connor enjoyed doing things that helped him to 'notice' what his body was doing – like taking his pulse when he was sitting and then running around and seeing how fast he could make it go – and then how slow he could make it go by trying to slow down his breathing. We asked mum to teach him how to take his own pulse and then to notice times of the day when he was relaxed – like first thing in the morning when he woke up. He and mum would take his pulse and then 'notice' the other signals his body was giving him to let him know that he was calm and relaxed.

Other ideas to build bodily awareness using the tactile system involve using touch in different ways. This needs to be done very carefully and bearing in mind what the child's previous experience of touch might have been. So, for example, if a child has been physically abused, it might take a long time of just doing very predictable hugs and perhaps very simple strokes down their back before the child is ready to tolerate some of the games suggested below. Remember that you'll need to tune into how the child is reacting each time that you try something, how they react today might be different to how they reacted yesterday. Touch that send your child into a fight or flight state of mind isn't going to be helpful.

When the child is comfortable with you touching them these are some ideas for games using touch:

» Rolling ball – ask the child to lie on their tummy and close their eyes. Run a ball down their backs, from their head to their feet. The first time you do this, go slowly and give a running commentary – I'm starting at the very top of your head…down over your hair…now I'm leaving your head and on your neck, moving down past your shoulder blades, ribs and spine...over your bottom and onto your legs – down your thighs, across your knees then down your calves towards your feet. Now I'm on the soles of your feet, can you feel it? If the child likes this, they might just enjoy you doing it over and over again. If you think they're ready to make it a bit harder you can tell them that you're going to change the game, this time stopping somewhere in between their head and their feet and see if they can tell you where you've stopped. When you first do this activity, start with a ball that's reasonably heavy, like a tennis ball or something that's very easy for them to feel. As they get better at it you can move onto things that are lighter and more difficult to feel – like a ping pong ball or even a (clean) feather duster!

» Back drawings – if the child is comfortable with the feeling of you touching them, whether it's through clothing or on their bare skin, it can be fun to draw shapes or letters on their back and see if they can guess what they are. It's important to build on success, so start with very easy lines and shapes, or things that can be easily distinguished from each other. So saying to the child 'I'm going to draw something on your back – can you guess if it's a sunshine or a clap of thunder' would be a good place to start. As the child gets better at distinguishing different shapes you can move on to more elaborate pictures.

Some children will be completely freaked out by this sort of activity and you'll need to adapt it so that it's well within their comfort zone. For some children this might mean doing something where they can see what you're doing – like a drawing on the palm of their hand – until they're feeling comfortable and safe with your touching them and able to relax and know it's a game that's fun. From there you could perhaps move to tracing the pattern of something on their arm or suggest that they close their eyes. Children who have been sexually abused may have some very unhelpful associations with touch and it may be that you'll need to get some help about how to proceed with this with these children.

Connor – the next steps

Once Connor had begun to be able to tune into his body and how it was feeling, we began to introduce exercises that were geared towards strengthening the discriminative arm of his tactile system. We were trying to help Connor move from the protective function of his tactile system that was geared to safety (and that he'd needed to protect himself as a small child) to one in which there was more room for exploration (now that he was safe and there were people who could take care of him and make sure that he was OK). We played games with 'feely bags' – drawstring cloth bags filled with all sorts of everyday objects like keys, a piece of Lego, a toy car, a golf ball or a rubber band. Connor had to put his hand into the bag and try and guess what the objects were, without using his eyes.

Some children find this quite tricky and it's important to think about grading it so that the child is successful. Remember the important bit is that the child is in a state of mind where they feel safe and happy. If the task is too hard or they're too worried about failing, they're going to move quickly into a state of fight or flight.

To make it easier you could get the child to choose objects to put into the bag and then see if they can find them or have an identical object outside the bag so that the child can see what they're looking for.

To make it harder you could put things in the bag that are trickier to identify – it's easier to find something like a key that's hard and has definite edges than it is to tell that a soft piece of fabric is a mitten. Another option is to make two bags with identical contents and the child has to find the same object in both bags.

We found that as Connor built up these 'foundation' sorts of skills, other things seemed to fall into place a bit for him. School reported him seeming more relaxed in himself and found that he was better able to cope with working in a pair or small group. He seemed more able to concentrate and they noticed improvements in his reading. At home there were more good times, with fewer violent outbursts and an increasing tolerance for playing games without always winning.

This wasn't the end of Connor's difficulties, but it gave us a good enough platform to begin to offer therapy. Connor was able to use therapy to sort out some of his early memories and the muddles in his mind at a time when he was experiencing some success at home and at school. This was good not only because it made it much easier to think about some of the things that were difficult for him, but also because the improved relationships at home meant that his foster parents were much better able to support him through the process helpfully. These are good illustrations of a graded approach to an activity – breaking things down into small manageable steps that the child can succeed at and progress through. This is particularly useful when working with children who can be in quite different states of mind from one day to the next for no apparent reason. The advantage of this sort of stepped approach is that it's really easy to go back to the step below if the child is struggling with something they could manage easily a few days ago.

Another guiding principle that goes alongside this is that it's best to start somewhere the child feels comfortable and build some associations and connections before moving on to something the child is struggling with.

Building vestibular and proprioceptive functioning

Before we think about the specifics of building vestibular and proprioceptive functioning, it's worth investing some time in doing a bit of troubleshooting.

Think heavy!

You may find that when you start doing some of these activities with your child they get a bit giddy or over aroused, so we need to start by working out how to calm them down again. This is where we can make good use of the proprioceptive system with activities that make some demand on the shoulder and pelvic girdle, like pushing against something heavy (e.g. moving furniture) or carrying a box of books, which tend to be calming to the central nervous system.

Things that involve a lot of quite hard effort are likely to be calming and to help to settle the child. Press ups are good, but children who have low muscle tone will find them hard. Wall squats are much easier to start with. For wall squats the child stands with their back against the wall and their feet out in front and then bends their knees until there are 90 degree angles between the hips and the knee and the knees and the feet. The child has to hold that position for as long as they can. It's quite hard – try it yourself! The temptation is to make it easier by going down lower but this defeats the object – it's meant to be hard! School can find this sort of activity helpful too. If a child is going to have to sit and do some writing or something that involves quite small, fine work (remember things like writing that happen a long way from the core of the body are hardest – like the arm of the crane) or need help in settling back into the classroom after the excitement of the playground, it can be useful to do some heavy proprioceptive work.

Some teachers are good at recognising the need for children to have breaks from certain activities, but miss out on the calming effect some heavy proprioceptive work could have. It can be helpful if the teacher keeps a box of heavy (but not too heavy!) books that quite often need to be taken along to either the secretary's office or to another classroom. This is a good proprioceptive activity and the child also gets points for being helpful! The secretary almost always has another box of books that need taking back into the classroom, so there's even more good stimulation for the system, which should help to get the child into a good, calm state of mind for work.

Outside school, some older children find swinging in a hammock (perhaps while listening to some soothing music) calming. Younger children need to be well supervised but the repetitive motion of swinging on a swing or rocking in a chair can be calming. The three important principles to remember in this section are:

Repeated patterns of movement when a child feels safe and happy are best for building new connections within the brain.

A graded or stepped approach works best.

Build associations when the child is feeling safe and happy and use these to help the child with things they are struggling with.

Let's think again about Zoe and the work we still had to do to get her into a state of mind where she was feeling safe and happy. We wanted to be confident that we were giving her movement experiences while she was in a state of mind that would allow her to stay in the movement of the experience and make good connections and memories (parasympathetic arm of the autonomic nervous system).

Zoe – building associations

Remember Zoe and how wobbly she was when she was sitting at a table trying to draw? Zoe's proprioceptive, vestibular and tactile functioning were all very poor. But Zoe's early abusive experiences meant that a lot of the activities that might normally be helpful to a child with poor functioning would remind her too much of touch and pressure that was scary. Instead of helping to build function, it would keep her in a fight or flight state (for Zoe this was either being hyperaroused or quite shut down). The challenge is often to try and find ways of getting a child like Zoe into a calm, happy state and then start to build things up from the beginning – the bottom of our building blocks. To do this it can be helpful to find an activity that the child is comfortable and happy with and build things up from there.

At one stage of our work together, we wanted to get Zoe sitting on her foster mum's knee on a rocking chair while mum was reading her a story. Zoe didn't really like sitting on her mum's knee for more than a nanosecond nor the feeling of rocking, so we knew that we had to take things slowly and go carefully. We had to work out when Zoe was happiest and how we could use this. Mum thought that the time of day that Zoe most often felt happy and relaxed was bath time. She would enjoy sitting and playing in the bath for much longer than she could sit and play out of the bath. We decided to use this as the time to build some good associations and connections so that we could use these when trying to build skills that were more difficult.

We started by playing some music that Zoe liked while she was in the bath. We played it quite quietly at first so as not to overwhelm her and gradually increasing the volume until she noticed it and began to enjoy having it on while she was in the bath. We were building associations between a time when she felt safe and happy – in the bath – with something she liked – the music.

As with all children, Zoe had bad days as well as good days. On a really bad day even bath time could be stressful and nothing could help make it any better. On those days mum didn't use the music – she didn't want to build associations between upset feelings and the music. She got really good at tuning into when Zoe was happy or relaxed and introducing associations and connections that she could then use to help Zoe with things she was finding difficult.

We then started putting that music on when mum and Zoe were in the rocking chair together. At first they'd just sit together and listen to the music, rocking gently. It took a few weeks for Zoe to sit for the length of one of the short songs, but mum took it very slowly, making sure that Zoe could get off whenever she wanted to so that she never got into that over-aroused state. Sometimes an additional incentive (like eating a favourite snack) was necessary to get Zoe to sit for long enough that she might begin to enjoy the motion of rocking. Gradually Zoe was beginning to relax and enjoy being with mum on the rocking chair and after some time they could listen to the whole CD together. Once they had reached this point, mum made sure that she had a (short) book with her on the chair and she would just gently suggest that they might look at the pictures while they were listening to the music or even just have the book on their knee. It was really important at each stage of this to monitor Zoe's reaction carefully and make changes so that she stayed in a 'comfort zone' – we didn't want to get the sympathetic nervous system activated otherwise we would lose the potential to be storing these new, good experiences. Mum was very good at tuning in to how Zoe was feeling and if she noticed that Zoe wasn't settled one day, she would just take things back a stage or go back to rocking a bit more to try to soothe and settle her.

Doing things like this allowed Zoe to build up some good early movement experiences and also to develop her relationship with mum in a very non-threatening way. There was no forced eye contact or having to show that she was enjoying a cuddle – reading a book helped to dilute the intensity of the situation and began to develop those good connections between the amygdala and frontal lobe.

As mum got better at judging what state of mind Zoe was in and build associations around the good times, we were able to start to build proprioceptive function.

———— Zoe – building proprioceptive skills

As with the little boy who put the garden fork through his foot because he didn't know where it was, we had to go right back to the beginning with Zoe to try and build up her map of her body. We started by playing a version of Simon Says with Zoe and either mum or dad lying on their back. We did it this way because it meant that she got most proprioceptive feedback about where her body was – she could feel her head, back, arms and leg against the floor and didn't have to look to see what they were doing. To begin with the instructions were very simple, like put your chin on your chest, shrug your shoulders (remembering that gaining bodily control is a top-down process – head, then neck, shoulder, trunk, hips and legs), and once she was competent at those they moved on to bending one leg, bending both legs, lifting one foot off the floor, etc. The next stage was to do things that involved her crossing over from one side of her body to the other – initially things like touch one ear with your other arm or touch your nose with one knee – and then moving on to rolling over onto her tummy, then pushing herself onto her feet and hands from there (like a bridge) and standing up.

From here they would build up to more complicated and co-ordinated things, like standing on one leg, hopping, marching, jumping and skipping. Because there was a danger of Zoe thinking it was a bit babyish and getting bored, they found music that went with the different stages and made it into a lot of fun!

It's easy to see how this mimics normal development and here we see how the systems become more intertwined. From lying on its back, a baby needs to spend time on its tummy and then support itself on to knees and hands before launching into crawling.

What to work on

While it's helpful to be able to try and work out whether a child's difficulties are more within the vestibular system or the proprioceptive/tactile systems, from my own experience of working with children who have been abused and neglected, I would say that it's often good to go back and do it all! Sometimes it's quite easy to tell where their difficulties lie. Children with proprioceptive problems often hold themselves quite rigidly – they can't control their movements very easily so they tense everything up to try and get some control. Remember to think of the proprioceptive system as being like the arm of the crane. These children often bump into things or trip over a lot. Children with poor postural control tend to use hard surfaces to orientate and balance themselves – perhaps sliding along a wall as the walk beside it. They can seem quite floppy and might be quite fearful of movement or do lots of crashing/banging and careering around. One way to get a bit of an idea of a child's vestibular functioning is to ask the child to lie down on their tummy with their arms stretched out in front of them (a bit like superman). Look at how well they're able to hold that position.

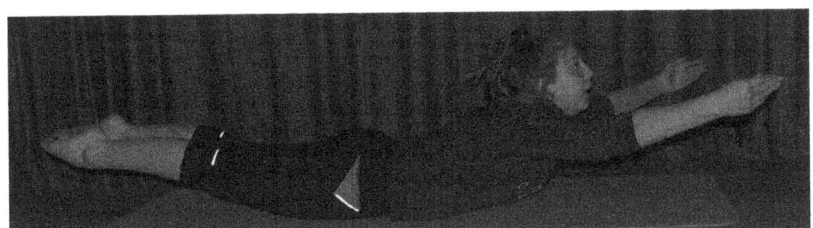

Usually by about the time they are eight, children with a good functioning vestibular system can get into and hold this position pretty well. Children who've missed out on the sorts of early movement experiences that build the vestibular system can't get into the position or tend to curl up and roll over onto their backs a bit like those fortune teller fish you get in Christmas crackers.

Another way to have a rough idea of how well the child's vestibular system is working is to ask the child to stand still and close their eyes and then hold that position for a minute. You're trying to see how well they're able to maintain their balance (postural control) without using their eyes. Try it yourself – it's surprisingly tricky. This gives useful information about the different systems, but it's very important to remember that if a child's vestibular system is very underdeveloped they're likely to find swinging or spinning movements make them feel quite sick or dizzy, and this isn't the state we want them to be in.

Activities

Children who have poor proprioceptive or vestibular functioning will benefit from lots of activities that build up the muscles that help them to stand tall and have some control over their limbs. This is postural control. When you're trying to plan how to do this, bear in mind how this control develops in babies and small children. From lying on their backs and moving their arms and legs, babies roll over onto their tummies and it's this time on their tummies that really build these systems. With babies, it's good to try and make their time on their tummies interesting enough for them to want to stay in that position – sometimes getting them to lie on your tummy or using a yoga ball can help to make it more fun and keep them interested and enjoying it.

Children who struggle to get into the superman position, (lying on their tummies with their legs and shoulders outstretched and off the ground) can sometimes find it easier to hold this position on a yoga ball, especially if the ball is a bit soft so that they can sink into it. This offers them a bit of stability that their bodies don't give them yet. Helping a child to hold this position on the ball is a good way of beginning to build this system. Then, as they get a bit more stable, you can inflate the ball a bit more, hold on to their legs or feet and gently roll them back and forward on the ball. As they get a bit better at this they'll be able to use their arms and hands to balance themselves and begin to do this themselves. It can be fun to make this into a game, perhaps putting a ball or bean bag a short distance in front of the ball and helping them to move towards it, all the time keeping their body and legs as straight as can be. You want to try and avoid them bending their legs – they should try and keep a straight line from their head down through their shoulders, torso and legs.

Slightly older children can be encouraged to lie on their tummies for short times – reading a book, colouring in or watching TV are all ideal. It may be that there needs to be some incentive to make this a more attractive prospect – often someone lying beside them helps or perhaps a bowl of something they enjoy eating.

Once they've become more comfortable in this position, it can be more fun for them to do more challenging things. Some children enjoy sliding down a slide on their tummies, and when they're feeling a bit more adventurous a water slide at the end of the slide can be really good fun.

Another example of gradually developing good vestibular and proprioceptive skills might look like this:

Step 1

Starting with basics, we want the child to develop a bit of head control when lying on their tummy and to build their shoulder girdle muscles. A good position for this is lying on their tummy propped up on their elbows. This isn't a particularly natural position, especially if the child isn't used to it. It's often helpful to start with short bursts and to have them do an activity while they're in this position (not least because it takes their mind off what they're doing). Remember, it's the lying on their tummy that we want to develop, so make sure that the activity is something they like and find easy so that they're in a calm, relaxed state. Colouring in or watching a favourite TV programme can work well.

Step 2

Next, try commando crawling (using elbows to propel). It's important to get the children using their arms to propel themselves. If a child has poor proprioceptive functioning they'll often try and use their knees to make themselves move, but it's really the shoulder and neck muscles that we want to develop here so encourage them to keep their legs straight and still. Building races and obstacle courses (perhaps over a pile of cushions, round the sofa and back to the start line) can make it more fun and perhaps keep the child engaged in something that will probably be quite difficult, at least initially.

Step 3

Once the child has developed a bit of control in this way, you can start to make it a bit more challenging. Occupational Therapists use scooter boards, which are like big skateboards, that the children lie on their tummies on and whizz around on, propelling themselves with their arms. There are lots of games that the child can play like this, from simple things like navigating a course around obstacles to playing ball games like passing and shooting goals with other children. Some people improvise scooter boards using skateboards but they're not as comfy or stable so need careful supervision.

From here things can start to get even more challenging. Wheelbarrows are a good way to go – you might remember these from your childhood. The child forms the wheelbarrow – they put their hands on the ground with straight arms at 90 degrees to their body, you hold their (straight) outstretched legs and the child uses their hands to walk forward. Perhaps to start with you'll need to hold their legs a bit higher up, more towards their hips, or just above their knees, if they're a bit wobbly and unstable. As always, you're wanting it to be fun and for the child to succeed, and a wheelbarrow isn't much fun if you can't control your tummy and legs enough to make good progress.

Once the child has become adept at this, you can make it more fun by having wheelbarrow races or setting timed challenges around the house. From here anything is possible – forward rolls, handstands, cartwheels, scooting...

It might be tempting to think that by taking your child to the play park you're covering all the sorts of experiences that we've talked about in this book. While the play parks offer lots of good opportunities to 'feed' sensory experiences, it's really important to remember the limbic system and the importance of the child feeling safe and happy while they're doing the movements, so that you're feeding the part of their brain that will be building memories and good associations. It's also a good opportunity to have time with your child, doing something together that can help to develop their relationship with you. Doing these activities should be fun – if they stop being fun then take a break. Starting at home works best, and then things can be transferred to the wider world once good, basic skills have been acquired.

In terms of sport, activities that require quite a lot of force, like badminton, are easier than games that uses a hard ball, like tennis or football, as it is much less noticeable if they overshoot with their movements. Things that offer quite a lot of resistance are usually good, like digging and making sandcastles out of wet sand.

In general, doing proprioceptive activities – like pushing, pulling, carrying heavy things, commando crawling – are the best places to start if you're unsure of how much vestibular functioning your child has. Don't start with spinning, swinging or bouncing – we don't want to over stimulate the child. And it's really important to keep watching and monitoring their reaction to anything they're doing. If you see your child seeming to startle or lose focus, just stop, take a break and see where you are before thinking about starting again. Lots of repeated patterns of experience are the key, but these can be quite short bursts.

Once children have a basic foundation in bodily awareness and regulation, it may be possible for them to go to community-based classes. Better regulation means that activities that the child has been too unsettled for become possible. Things like gymnastics, horse riding, music and movement classes, drumming, children's yoga and swimming are all really useful.

Movement experiences in a safe and happy environment build the best neural pathways, so it's important to give some thought to how to make these sorts of activities fun for children. While commando crawling on its own isn't much fun, putting it into a different context can make it more exciting.

The following activities give some ideas for making the kind of movements we're wanting our children to do more interesting. Have fun developing and changing them – they're really designed to give you some ideas to get started.

The first one, 'Treasure Island', calls for a 'friend' towards the end (that can be you!) and some 'tasty treasure'. I usually find a stash of chocolate coins saved from Christmas works well!

Treasure island

You've just been thrown overboard and managed to swim to an island – you crawl up out of the waves (commando crawling) and have to pull yourself over rocks and boulders (piles of cushions) using only your arms. You reach a cave and find a box of blankets that's been washed up.

You lift the (heavy) box and carry it to a good space where you decide to build a den for the night. You use all the blankets and covers in the box to make a really good den for yourselves.

It's really cold, so once your den has been built you have to wrap up tight in blankets to keep warm. You lie on your tummy near the door of the den so that you can keep a good look out for any wild animals that might be nearby.

In the morning…

You wake up starving hungry but are still being very cautious. You crawl under rocks (cushions, blankets) and manage to reach a cave. You catch your leg on a sharp rock and can't crawl any more. Luckily your friend is strong and can help you wheelbarrow walk. Just when you're thinking you've got no more energy you come across some treasure – a box of yummy…

Mountain Rescue

First you need to build your base camp. Use material and duvets to make a snug little campsite for yourself (a little pop-up tent is handy too and can be filled with cushions and blankets to make it cosier). It's freezing outside and you snuggle down into your sleeping bag.

You lie on your back. You can't get comfy so you flip over onto your tummy to see if that's better. No better. Back onto your bed. And again onto your tummy.

Then you hear a scratching sound. Is it a mouse? A deer? You know that you can't get out of your sleeping bag because you'll freeze to death but you have to find out what's there. Staying tightly wrapped in your sleeping bag you crawl like a caterpillar to the door of your tent. Looking out you think you can see something and decide to explore a bit more. You throw the duvet out of the tent to make a path for yourself and slide along it, trying to be silent and stealthy. It's getting warmer now and you slip out of your sleeping bag and throw the duvet ahead of you.

This time you try to crawl under the duvet, keeping well out of sight. What you've forgotten is that you pitched your tent at the top of the hill and now you find yourself rolling over and over down the hill…

You land in a pile of soft heather (cushions) and stand up to make sure you're OK. You stamp your feet and do a few star jumps just to check everything's working. There's a path through a field (cushions) that you have to pick your way through carefully – it's really boggy so try to stay on the cushions…

Conclusion

When we think about long-term impact of trauma and neglect on children, we usually draw on two main theories, namely attachment and trauma.

Bringing sensory integration into the equation adds helpful insight into why it's also important to pay attention to the kinds of movement experiences that are often missed for these babies and children. Using the idea of sequential development, sensory integration allows us to take the child back through essential patterns of movement that have been missed. By building these underlying systems, we're really going back and re-laying the foundations, rebuilding the child's sense of themselves. Once a child is more in touch with and connected to themselves on a bodily level, all sorts of things fall into place. Being involved in the process of re-laying these foundation movements allows parents to be part of the child becoming re-connected with themselves in a way that reflects what happens for typically developing children in a secure attachment relationship. From here the child is in a much better position to be able to connect with the people in their world which in turn forms a platform for the development of the skills for thinking and learning. This can also be a good time to start play or talking based therapies.

None of us particularly like doing things that don't come easily to us, and it's the same when we're thinking about trying to build a child's system that's not been well enough primed. A child who has weak shoulder girdle muscles will probably have developed lots of ways of compensating for this by using other parts of their body – the way Zoe did when she clamped her whole arm against the side of her body to give her enough stability to write. Persuading children to use parts of their body that are less well-developed requires careful thinking. Hopefully the ideas in the book around building associations and grading activities will help to keep things fun and engaging. Keep thinking about what state of mind the child's in and don't worry about abandoning something one day if it doesn't seem to be going well – you can always try again later, or approach it from a different angle. Pitching the activities at the right level for the child means they should have more success and this in turn builds confidence and helps children to try the next level of things. As children begin to get stronger and their movements become more fluid, their confidence in their skills grows and this helps to propel them onwards. Hopefully you and your child together will find new and interesting games and ideas that work towards the goal you're aiming for. Have fun!

RECOMMENDED READING

About sensory integration

These books go into more detail about the different systems but are mainly concerned with children with sensory processing disorders rather than the group of children we've been talking about:

- *Sensory Integration and the Child* by Dr A Jean Ayres – Jean Ayres was the pioneer of Sensory integration and this book brings together lots of her ideas.

- *Raising a Sensory Smart Child* by Lindsey Biel and Nancy Peske and *The Out of Synch Child* by Carol Stock Kranowitz – these books both give lots of practical exercises to do with children to help build their sensory systems and talk about a balanced sensory diet.

Éadaoin Bhreathnach is the exception to this – she's an Occupational Therapist who has developed the Sensory Attachment Intervention, which explores the links between sensory integration, attachment and self-regulation.

- Adoption UK Article – Sensory Attachment Intervention: *www.sensoryattachmentintervention. com/Documents/Adoption%20UK%20Article.pdf*

- Bhreathnach, E. and Bhreathnach, S. (2011) *The Scared Gang.* Boolino: Alder Tree Press.

About trauma and attachment

- *The Boy who was Raised as a Dog* by Bruce Perry – a really easy to read but informative book that uses case examples to illustrate the impact of trauma on the developing child. There is a website too, Child Trauma Academy (http://childtrauma.org), which, while it's written from a US perspective, has a wealth of information and links to online talks and lectures.

- *Nurturing Natures* by Graham Music – this book has lots of information about normal development, trauma and attachment.

- Perry, B.D. (2008) 'Child Maltreatment: A Neurodevelopmental Perspective on the Role of Trauma and Neglect in Psychopathology.' In *Child and Adolescent Psychopathology.* Hoboken, NJ: John Wiley & Sons, pp.93–129.

- Maguire, E.A., Woollett, K. and Spiers, H.J. (2006) 'London taxi drivers and bus drivers: a structural MRI and neuropsychological analysis.' *Hippocampus 16,* 12, 1091–101.

About fostering and adoption

- *A Child's Journey Through Placement* by Vera Fahlberg – a great book, full of ideas about child development and helping children to settle into placement.

- *New Families, Old Scripts* by Caroline Archer and Christine Gordon – this is written by foster carers and is aimed at helping foster and adoptive parents to understand a child's behaviour and begin to change it – they talk about understanding the language of trauma being the first step to being able to make change happen.

- *Real Parents, Real Children* by Holly van Gulden and Lisa Bartels-Rabb – this considers the challenges of adopting children of different ages and how to help them to become part of your family.

- There are lots of independent fostering and adoption agencies whose websites have great information and ideas about all sorts of issues and challenges that are relevant to both fostering and adoption. This is definitely not an exhaustive list, but the Coram, Pac-UK, TACT and Adoption UK sites are all helpful.

  » Coram UK
    www.coram.org.uk
    02075200300

» PAC-UK
www.pac-uk.org
London: 020 7284 0555
Leeds: 01132646837

» TACT
http://tactcare.org.uk/
020 3582 5378

» Adoption UK
www.adoptionuk.org
08448487900

GLOSSARY

Amygdala – part of the limbic system, really important in processing emotions and making links between the thinking part of the brain – cerebral cortex and the parts of the body that prepare us for immediate action (fight or flight). It's the amygdala that 'weighs up' an experience and works with the rest of the limbic system in deciding how to respond.

Autonomic nervous system – there are two 'arms' to the autonomic nervous system (sympathetic and parasympathetic) that decide how the body will react to a situation.

Brainstem – the brainstem is concerned with important physiological functions like heart rate, breathing, blood pressure and digestion. Sometimes referred to in books about trauma as the 'reptilian brain' to reflect its presence in creatures like tortoises and reptiles that don't have a higher thinking (cerebral cortex) part of their brain. When people are in a fight or flight state of mind they're sometimes referred to as working from their reptilian brain, because they're not able to make use of the higher functioning/thinking parts of their brain.

Central nervous system – the collective name for the brain and spinal cord. The central nervous system receives information from within the body and outside the body and uses this information to make sense of the world and be able to plan, move, think and relate.

Cerebral cortex – the 'higher functioning' part of the brain, concerned with concentration, problem solving, creative ideas, problem solving and impulse control.

Cortisol – commonly known as the stress hormone because when the body is in a fight or flight state, more cortisol is released. Under everyday conditions, when the threat or danger has passed, cortisol levels can return to normal, but this may not be the case for children or people living with a lot of stress a lot of the time.

Endocrine system – this is the name for the collection of glands that produce hormones. These hormones may be concerned with all sorts of functions, but an important one when thinking about trauma is cortisol.

Hippocampus – another part of the limbic system, the hippocampus is really important in the making and storing of memories. It's the hippocampus that links with the endocrine system to switch off the stress hormone cortisol.

Hypothalamus – part of the limbic system the hypothalamus works alongside the amygdale and hippocampus and controls the autonomic nervous system. The hypothalamus has lots of connections with the endocrine system which. Amongst other things, triggers the release of the stress hormone cortisol.

Impulse control – being able to stop and think before reacting to something.

Limbic system – the collective name for the amygdala, hippocampus and hypothalamus. Its job is to link the parts of the brain that are concerned with physiological functioning like heart rate, breathing and digestion, with the higher thinking areas (cerebral cortex). The limbic system works outside of conscious awareness.

Occulomotor functioning – good occulomotor functioning is one of the tasks of the vestibular system, and is concerned with the connection between our eyes and movement. An example of good occulomotor functioning is being able to drive over bumpy ground and have your visual field remain stable.

Otoliths – part of the vestibular system, the otoliths are receptors in the ears and are stimulated by linear movements like being rocked. The otoliths send messages down the spine to the muscles in the neck and body that are concerned with being able to stand up tall and have good posture.

Parasympathetic nervous system – part of the autonomic nervous system. When there is an absence of threat or stress, the parasympathetic nervous system keeps things calm and at a level of arousal that's best suited to being able to take things in, remember and learn. If a child is very stressed, it's the sympathetic nervous system that's going to be controlling.

Postural control – being able to stand tall, stay well balanced and have a strong core.

Proprioceptive system – this is the system that's all about the smooth, well co-ordinated working of the muscle groups that extend (lengthen) and contract (shorten) the muscles. The proprioceptive system gets feedback from the joints and muscles and all of this information is used to decide how much pressure or force to use in a movement. Sometimes if you're given a hug by a child with very poor proprioceptive functioning it might feel as if you don't know if you're being hugged or squeezed much too hard. If the vestibular system is like the base of the crane, the proprioceptive system is like its arm.

Regulation – being able to get things 'just right' and adjust your level of arousal to the situation. Regulation can mean different things in different situations – in an exam situation it would be staying calm enough to be able to focus and answer the questions. On a football pitch, a well regulated player would be able to keep control of themselves and not be too loud, not go too fast so that he overshot the ball, not be too jerky or floppy when s/he was kicking the ball.

Semi-circular canals – part of the vestibular system, the semi-circular canals are the receptors in the ears that detect rotator movements. An activity like doing roly-poly down a hill or doing a handstand would be very stimulating for this part of the vestibular system

Sensory integration – originally described by Occupational Therapist A. Jean Ayres, sensory integration theory offers a way of understanding how the brain and body processes and stores experiences, on an emotional and physical level.

Sensory processing – a way of describing how the brain and central nervous system make sense of the input they receive from inside and outside the body and use this to plan and carry out our actions

Sensory processing disorder – a broad description of difficulties in the planning or execution of movements. Something like dyspraxia would come under the umbrella of a sensory processing disorder.

Somatosensory system – a word that's commonly used in sensory integration books to describe the proprioceptive and tactile systems together.

Sympathetic nervous system – part of the autonomic nervous system, the sympathetic nervous system is responsible for the 'fight or flight' reaction. In this state, the child is unlikely to be able to process and absorb new learning or good experiences – the body's whole focus is on survival.

Tactile system – this system is concerned with touch in all its forms. The receptors for the tactile system are on the outside of the body. Different areas of the body have different sorts of touch receptors, which may be to register pain, pleasure, temperature or discriminate between different textures.

Vestibular system – the first system to form while the baby is in the womb, the vestibular system is like the body of a crane – it keeps us steady and grounded so that we have a sense of bodily security and grounded-ness. The receptors for the vestibular system are in the ears and are the otoliths and semi-circular canals. Like the proprioceptive and tactile systems, the vestibular system needs lots of movement experiences from birth onwards to work at its best. Children with poor functioning vestibular systems can often be quite floppy, have poor balance and co-ordination or have a fearfulness about movement – e.g. if they were put onto a trampoline they might want to stay very close to the mat rather than jumping around, or might be fearful and wanting to hang on tight at the top of a flight of stairs.

INDEX